Sinner Ella

A Gospel Pantomime

Michael Forster

Kevin Mayhew

First published in 1999 by
KEVIN MAYHEW LTD
Buxhall
Stowmarket
Suffolk IP14 3DJ

© 1999 Michael Forster

The right of Michael Forster to be identified as the author
of this work has been asserted by him in accordance
with the Copyright, Designs and Patents Act 1988.

All rights reserved. No part of this publication may
be reproduced, stored in a retrieval system, or transmitted,
in any form or by any means, electronic, mechanical,
photocopying, recording or otherwise,
without the prior written permission of the publisher.

The drama sections of this book may be photocopied
by the church or organisation purchasing it
without copyright infringement, provided they
are used for the purpose for which they are intended.
Reproduction of any of the contents of this book
for commercial purposes is subject to
the usual copyright restrictions.

0 1 2 3 4 5 6 7 8 9

ISBN 1 84003 387 8
Catalogue No 1500283

Cover by Darren
Edited by Elisabeth Bates
Typesetting by Richard Weaver
Printed in Great Britain

First published in 1999 by
KEVIN MAYHEW LTD
Buxhall
Stowmarket
Suffolk IP14 3DJ

© 1999 Michael Forster

The right of Michael Forster to be identified as the author
of this work has been asserted by him in accordance
with the Copyright, Designs and Patents Act 1988.

All rights reserved. No part of this publication may
be reproduced, stored in a retrieval system, or transmitted,
in any form or by any means, electronic, mechanical,
photocopying, recording or otherwise,
without the prior written permission of the publisher.

The drama sections of this book may be photocopied
by the church or organisation purchasing it
without copyright infringement, provided they
are used for the purpose for which they are intended.
Reproduction of any of the contents of this book
for commercial purposes is subject to
the usual copyright restrictions.

0 1 2 3 4 5 6 7 8 9

ISBN 1 84003 387 8
Catalogue No 1500283

Cover by Darren
Edited by Elisabeth Bates
Typesetting by Richard Weaver
Printed in Great Britain

Sinner Ella

A Gospel Pantomime

Michael Forster

Kevin Mayhew

Foreword

A pantomime is for life – not just for Christmas! This show could be produced at any time of year as a fun way of presenting the gospel.

The well-known and loved pantomime *Cinderella* is about the liberating of the oppressed, which gives it a very strong resonance with the gospel. However, there are also crucial differences: the use of fairy-tale magic does not fit our understanding of the way God works, and the original story does nothing to address the fundamental injustice itself – Cinderella is simply enabled to become a member of the elite few, and the social snobbery is pandered to rather than challenged.

This show makes radical changes in both aspects. There is no 'Fairy Godmother' to transform Cinderella and pander to social norms; instead, Ella is encouraged to value herself *as she is*, and to attend the function in her everyday clothes, without the fairytale dress, coach etc. Because of this, the fundamental issue *is* addressed: Ella, in her present state, is valued while the trappings of her 'acceptable' stepsisters are exposed as the sham they really are. This is the God of *Magnificat*.

> He has shown strength with his arm; he has scattered the
> proud in the thoughts of their hearts. He has brought down
> the powerful from their thrones, and lifted up the lowly.
> (Luke 1:51-52 NRSV)

Our heroine, Ella, is very close to many people today who are burdened with irrational guilt. It is usually hard to find any real reason for it, often because there is none – guilt is a very powerful weapon by which the strong can exploit and dominate the weak (and all of us have probably used it at some time). The Christian gospel is meant to set people free from such abuses: since we are *all* sinners, saved only by the grace of God, there is no scope for our judging, labelling and abusing anyone else. It's interesting to note that Jesus' (sometimes positively vitriolic) words of denunciation were directed at those who considered themselves good, the religious élite, and not at those who felt guilty already.

This, then, is truly a 'gospel' pantomime: the Good News that liberates the oppressed. Hopefully, though, it's a few degrees less 'preachy' than that sentence! So, take the script and have fun with it: encourage all the usual pantomime responses, and pray that the love of Christ, who first accepts us as we are, and *then* offers us new, transformed life, will work through it.

Oh yes, he will!

MICHAEL FORSTER

The Story

The story is very close to *Cinderella*. 'Sinner' Ella lives with her unkind ugly stepsisters, Anaesthesia and Anaglypta, at Bourton Paidfor Hall – the stately home of Baron Spentup. She is ill treated, and kept in 'her' place by being made to feel guilty – although the sisters will never specify the nature of her 'sin' ('We don't want to talk about it'). Her only friend in the world, until the audience arrive, is Salome, her family's maid.

The sisters are excited because they are going to the 'Meet a Local Personality' night at their church, at which a local radio presenter, Josh Christian, is to be the star attraction. They have ambitions to be gospel singers and think meeting him will be their big break. Ella, of course, cannot go within miles of the church, but is despatched into the woods to gather firewood to heat the sisters' bathwater.

In the wood, Ella meets and befriends a woman, Mary, who turns out to be Josh's mother and encourages Ella to go to the church, exactly as she is. Ella takes a gift for Josh, – a bottle of perfume left to her by her late mother, and therefore very precious – but when she arrives her sense of guilt causes her to panic and she spills the contents of the bottle over the distinguished guest before rushing out in tears.

Josh is desperate to help Ella, and sets out to search for her. Eventually, it turns out that Josh is not the wealthy showbiz star the sisters had thought, but ploughs his resources into social projects working with people whom respectable society (and especially Anaesthesia and Anaglypta) finds repulsive. Suddenly he seems much less attractive to them, but Ella and Salome join him – leaving the Baron and his daughters without their skivvies. Now, one of them is going to have to take Ella's place – so upon whom will the mantle of manipulative guilt fall next?

CAST

SALOME
a maid

ELLA
ill-treated step-daughter of Baron Spentup

ANAESTHESIA
an ugly sister

ANAGLYPTA
an ugly sister

BARON SPENTUP
owner of Bourton Paidfor Hall

MARY
mother of Josh

SIMON
religious leader

FIRST CRONY

SECOND CRONY

JOSH

PIERS
Josh's road manager

Production Notes

As with the first Christian pantomime, *A lad in a manger*, simplicity is the key in all aspects of production. There is no reason why this show should be beyond the resources of an average or smaller church, youth club etc. However, this should not mean that special talents cannot be used; tailor the show to the resources available and allow people's particular skills to be valued without their feeling overstretched or threatened.

SETS

The three sets are: the kitchen at Bourton Paidfor Hall; the woods where Ella collects firewood and meets Mary; and the church where the social event is being held. The first and third of these are relatively simple, requiring merely a change of the notice on the wall. However, some simple furniture and a 'stove' probably made from a large cardboard carton, will be needed for the kitchen. The woods could cause difficulties if attempts are made to produce a full set – unless, of course, the necessary skills are among the talents you wish to affirm in members of your group. In that case, feel free to create elaborate but quickly changeable sets. Most churches, however, will not be able to do that, partly because of the nature of the building itself. In that case, the set could either be a minimalist, representative set, or you could use people: simple costumes of dark full-length dresses and hoods, with branches (real or otherwise) to hold in the hands, and you have a set that's capable of erecting and removing itself. All kinds of fun can be had with the trees: 'I'm sure I've seen that tree before somewhere – oh yes, the Mother's Union.' The trees could gently but menacingly wave their branches, adding a whole new atmosphere to the scene.

COSTUMES

The show is intended to be in modern dress. The ugly sisters could send up some of the more presentable excesses of the fashion industry, and Baron Spentup could be a caricature of a 'landed gent'. Josh and Piers are distinctly underdressed for the party, probably in T-shirts and jeans, making them more accessible to Ella than to Simon and his cronies who will, of course, be wearing the most socially pretentious kind of clothes.

DIALOGUE

I have provided the basic structure and dialogue, and this on its own would work well enough. However, in the true spirit of pantomime, the show will be best when you take it and make it your own: local references, 'in jokes', allusions perhaps to contemporary events, catch-phrases etc.

MUSIC

Pantomimes are not musicals, and songs play an important but small part in the overall effect. I have offered a few new lyrics set to old tunes for ease of learning. All the tunes for the songs, and the suggested incidental music, can be found in *Top Tunes* (Kevin Mayhew), and these could be played on a keyboard or whatever combination of instruments is available. Alternatively, you may well wish to substitute appropriate songs from, for example, the current hit parade in place of some of the ones suggested here. A karaoke machine would be a simple way to do that, but please ensure that appropriate permissions have been sought from the people who hold the rights on the works. God is not honoured in the flouting of copyright and performance rights law.

Another way of enhancing the show would be to use special tunes to identify different characters, rather in the style of the operatic *leitmotif*. A few bars of the tune could be played when the character enters. Here are some examples, all from *Top Tunes*.

- Ella   *Greensleeves*
- Ugly Sisters   *Dance of the Sugar Plum Fairy*
- Baron Spentup   *The Man who Broke the Bank at Monte Carlo*
- Mary   *Ave Maria (Schubert)*
- Josh   *Shaker Song*

Incidental music also plays an important part, especially in the more dramatic scenes. There are plenty of options and the only limitations are the available resources and imagination.

SOUND EFFECTS

These can really bring a pantomime to life, but must fit in with the action. If you have a suspended cymbal to strike when anybody falls over, that's good; if not, get someone to dangle a saucepan lid by a piece of string while someone else hits it. Experiment during rehearsal and let people bring their own imaginations to bear on it.

RABBLE-ROUSING

Audience involvement is obviously vital to a successful production, and it would be worth having one or two well prepared 'plants' seated anonymously at strategic places who could encourage this by heckling, joining in etc., at appropriate moments. Again, some suggestions are made in the script, and some of these would certainly need to be led; but do whatever is appropriate in your setting. And of course, ensure that the 'plants' are properly acknowledged when it comes to the time for the final curtain call.

BE FLEXIBLE!

As suggested earlier, unnecessary complication is best avoided; work within your own resources. However, this should not stifle initiative where particular talents exist. If, for example, you have a member who is an accomplished juggler, then find an excuse to get them on the stage! The party scene, for example, could be an opportunity to show off any talents people have. Simon won't approve at all, but Josh will love it! If you have more actors than the script allows for, then create a few more characters, but don't let people feel either press-ganged or excluded.

I hope you have lots of fun with this production – it's certainly been enjoyable to write – and that the essential Christian message, of God overcoming evil not by mere superior force but by the 'more excellent *way*' of love, will be well communicated in the process.

You could photocopy the poster opposite and get the children to colour it, add your own details of dates, venue etc., and display in prominent places around the area.

Sinner Ella

A Gospel Pantomime

Michael Forster

SCENE 1

The kitchen at Bourton Paidfor Hall. Sign on wall says 'Bourton Paidfor Hall. Comfy seat of Baron Spentup'.

Enter SALOME, looking around her. She catches sight of the audience.

Salome There you are! Thank goodness you've come. I wasn't sure if you'd get my message. Now, I've got you in here because I need your help. Well, actually it's my friend Ella who does. She's a really lovely person, and she doesn't deserve for people to be so rotten to her, but they are – especially those horrible stepsisters of hers. So what you've got to do is show her you love her. When she comes in, give a really big cheer. Can you do that?

Let's try

Oh, come on! Tell you what: imagine the Bee Gees* have just arrived.

That's better. Now when Ella comes, you do that. Got it? Good. Here she is.

Enter ELLA, who starts in surprise at the cheer.

Ella Salome, who are all these people?

Salome They're your friends.

Ella *(Glumly)* No they're not. I haven't got any.

Salome Oh yes you have!

Ella Oh no I haven't!

SALOME encourages the audience to take up the cry.

Salome There. See? And they've come from all over the place just to show you they care.

Ella Well, thank you, boys and girls. I'm really pleased, because until you came along I didn't have any friends here at all.

---

* Use whatever name is appropriate to the time and place.

Salome	Ahem! Ahem!
Ella	Except Salome, of course. She's my very best friend.
Anaesthesia	(*Offstage*) I say, has anybody seen my earrings?
Ella	(*Frightened*) Oh dear, that's Anaesthesia! Now I'm for it.
Salome	Why? Have *you* borrowed her earrings?
Ella	I wouldn't be seen dead in them, but you know Anaesthesia. I'm bound to get the blame.
Salome	Why are they getting all dolled up, anyway?
Ella	Haven't you heard? There's a big do on at the church. Josh Christian's coming.
Salome	Josh Christian! Not *the* Josh Christian – the man who does the gospel show on Radio Bradgate?*
Ella	Yes. Apparently the church have got him to do one of their 'Meet a Local Personality' evenings.
Salome	But what's that got to do with Anaesthesia and Anaglypta?
Ella	They're going. They think Josh is going to invite them to sing on his show.
Salome	*Them?!* Well, I suppose they do sing beautifully – compared with a pair of alley cats trapped in a dustbin with a rotweiller. You should go along. Now you *can* sing.
Ella	Oh, I couldn't go. Not a bad person like me. Not to the church.
Salome	Bad person like you! What makes you any worse than anyone else?
Ella	I don't know. No one will tell me but I must have done something dreadful for Anaglypta and Anaesthesia to hate me so much.

* Give it a local-sounding name.

Salome	They've got you right under control haven't they! They make you feel guilty and then you'll do whatever they want. Can't you see what they're up to?
Ella	Oh, no, I'm sure I must have done something. One day I'll remember.
Salome	I give up! *(Heavy footfalls offstage. SALOME turns to audience)* Here come the gruesome twosome, now. Can you boo as loudly as you can cheer? Get ready, then.

Enter ANAGLYPTA and ANAESTHESIA. They react to the booing.

Anaesthesia	Ooh, look, Anaglypta! The place is full of horrible children.
Anaglypta	Yes, that's strange. It's not Sunday morning, is it?*
Anaesthesia	Oh, no. The ones we have here then are horrible – but these are *mega* horrible.
Audience	Oh no we're not!
Anaesthesia	Oh yes you are!
Anaglypta	Ignore them, Anaesthesia
Anaesthesia	No, I've got a better idea. *(Smiles horribly)* Hello, children. Now, I'm Anaesthesia and this is my almost as beautiful sister, Anaglypta. Would you like to be our friends?
Audience	No!
Anaesthesia	Oh yes you would!
	Perhaps you're right, dear. Let's just ignore the horrible little monsters.
Anaglypta	They're only jealous of our stunning beauty, Anaesthesia.
Audience	Oh no we're not!
Anaglypta	Oh yes you are!

*This assumes a church production: change it if necessary to 'It's not term-time' or some other appropriate comment.

Anaesthesia	Ignore them, dear. Who cares about them when we've got each other?

SISTERS
Tune: *Daisy, Daisy*

Anaglypta	Sisters, sisters,
Anaesthesia	that's what we've always been.
Anaglypta	Sisters, sisters,
Anaesthesia	the sweetest you've ever seen.
Anaglypta	Our beauty is legendary,
Anaesthesia	we're quite extraordinary,
Anaglypta	and we're in demand, by the royal command,
Salome	every autumn, for Halloween!

ANAGLYPTA lashes out and SALOME dodges out of reach just in time.

Dialogue:

Anaglypta	Now, I'll need my best dress for the church. Josh will be dazzled by my beauty as well as my talent.
Anaesthesia	Of course, he may only need one new singer. So I hope you won't be too disappointed, *Anaglypta dear,* but I'll make sure you get a discount on tickets when we're on tour.
Anaglypta	And what tour would that be, *dearest* Anaesthesia?
Salome	You must be off your rockers, the pair of you.
Anaesthesia	As soon as he takes one look at me, he'll know the decision is made.
Anaglypta	*(Too sympathetically)* Yes, and I hope you won't be too hurt, dear.

Anaesthesia	*(Angrily)* You're the one who'll be hurt, if you get in my way.
Anaglypta	Shush, dear! *(Indicating audience)* Remember we're not alone!
Anaesthesia	Oops!

Song continues:

Anaglypta	Sisters, sisters,
Anaesthesia	we're never apart you know,
Anaglypta	like French and Saunders,
Ella	Jack and Jill,
Salome	wash and go.
Anaglypta	Through poverty, wind or weather, we'll always be together.
Anaesthesia	These faithful hearts will never part,
Salome	for they've got nowhere else to go.

ANAESTHESIA lashes out and SALOME dodges out of reach just in time.

Dialogue:

Anaglypta	We're so loving! And when I'm famous, I'll always be nice to my *poor*, less fortunate sister Anaesthesia.
Anaesthesia	You're not going to be famous! You keep your eyes off Josh, you underdeveloped moron, you – he's mine!
Salome	From what I hear, he isn't anybody's. You two really are away with the fairies, aren't you!
Anaglypta and Anaesthesia	*(Together, embracing each other as they speak)* Don't you talk to my darling sister like that!

Song continues:

Anaesthesia	Sisters, sisters, all that we've got we share.
Anaglypta	Sisters, sisters, showing how much we care.
Anaesthesia	We're mu-tu-al-ly supportive,
Salome	(They wear each other's corsets.)
Anaglypta	And we're always good, doing what we should,
Anaesthesia	and we don't commit sins, like her. *(Pointing to ELLA.)*
Ella	What have I done?
Anaesthesia	I don't want to talk about it.
Ella	You never want to talk about it, but how can I say sorry if I don't know what for?
Anaglypta	I'll give you what for, you horrible little child. Now stop snivelling and go and get lots of firewood for the boiler.
Anaesthesia	We need lots of hot water for our baths.
Anaglypta	And then, while we're having them, you can iron our new dresses and polish our jewellery ready for tonight.
Anaesthesia	We're going to make ourselves look devastatingly attractive.
Salome	What! In six short hours?
Ella	I wish *I* was going.
Anaesthesia	What! They don't allow *sinners* into the church.
Anaglypta	And Josh wouldn't be seen *dead* near someone like you.
Ella	But what have I done that's so terrible?
Anaesthesia	I don't want to talk about it.
Anaglypta	We *never* talk about it.

Ella	But –
Anaesthesia	No more! I can't bear to think about it. Now off you go you horrible little girl and get the firewood.

Exit ELLA.

Anaglypta	*(Calls after her)* And don't go talking to any nice people while you're out.
Salome	I'd better go with her – keep her company.
Anaesthesia	Oh, no you don't. You're supposed to be the upstairs maid. Go upstairs and get something made.
Anaglypta	That's right. Make the beds.
Anaesthesia	And the tea.
Anaglypta	And a fool of yourself.
Anaesthesia	Should come naturally.

Exit SALOME.

Enter BARON SPENTUP.

Anaesthesia	Oh, Father dear, how wonderful to see you.
Anaglypta	We've missed you dreadfully.
Baron	I've only been gone an hour.
Anaesthesia	But it seems so long.
Baron	All right, what do you want?
Anaglypta	Only an advance on our allowance.
Baron	You've just had an advance.
Anaesthesia	Not on our allowance for November next year but one, we haven't.
Anaglypta	And anyway, you haven't given us an increase since – ooh, *three months* ago!

Baron	Well, I'm sorry, my dears, but I just haven't got any money at present.
Anaesthesia	Same old story, they don't call you Baron Spentup for nothing.
Baron	Well it's certainly been true for the past – let's see, how old are you both now? – *(They frantically try to shush him)* forty-two years.
Anaesthesia	Oh, the shame!
Anaglypta	The indignity!
Baron	Anyway, you should be getting ready. Josh specialises in songs about new life, and goodness knows, you two could use it. So when he asks you what you want, what are you going to say?
Anaesthesia	*(Sweetly)* 'To help old people and be kind to animals'.
Anaglypta	*(Sweetly)* 'World peace and an end to poverty'.
Baron	And do try to sound as though you mean it.
Anaglypta	Oh, we do, we do!
Audience	Oh no you don't!
Anaesthesia	Oh yes we do!
Baron	Where's Ella?
Anaesthesia	Gone to collect firewood.
Salome	*(Aside to audience)* There's a couple of witches need burning.
Anaesthesia	What did you say?
Salome	I said she'd better be quick in returning.
Anaesthesia	She's been ages!
Anaglypta	Well, we can't wait here for ever. Come on, dear, let's go and do our nails.

Baron   You'll find your nail file in the stables – the blacksmith borrowed it this morning.

Exeunt ANAESTHESIA and ANAGLYPTA.

Baron   Daughters! Nothing but bother!

Exit

SCENE 2

The woods.

Enter ELLA carrying a small quantity of sticks.

Ella Oh, dear! I'm never going to find enough firewood at this rate. Anaesthesia and Anaglypta will be really angry.

Enter MARY, also looking for sticks, bending down with obvious difficulty to pick them up.

Ella I don't know why they're so horrible to me. No one will tell me what I'm supposed to have done. *(She catches sight of Mary)* Oh, let me help you. Come over here and sit down. *(She helps Mary over to a tree stump. MARY sits on it.)*

Mary Thank you very much, you're really kind.

You've been crying!

Ella Oh, it's nothing – really.

Mary If it's enough for you to cry about, it's not nothing. Why not tell me?

Ella It's all my own fault. I'm a bad person and everybody hates me – well, everybody except Salome, anyway.

Mary What have you done?

Ella I don't know. They won't tell me.

Mary Oh, I see. They just make you feel guilty, so that you always do as they tell you.

Ella You sound as if you know what it's like.

Mary Believe me, I do – it's a very old trick. My name's Mary, by the way. What's yours?

Ella Ella. But everyone calls me *Sinner* Ella.

Mary	Well, *I'll* just call you Ella. You remind me of me, when I was young. The neighbours all gossiped about me, too, although I hadn't done anything wrong at all. But they wouldn't believe me.
Ella	Did they shut *you* out of things, too?
Mary	Sometimes. Like what, especially?
Ella	The church are having a 'Meet a Local Personality' night. Both my stepsisters are going but I'm not allowed. Josh Christian's going to be there and I certainly can't go near *him*.
Mary	Well, if you want my advice: ignore them. Go to the church and meet Josh. You'll find him a lot more human than you expect.
Ella	You know him, then?
Mary	Know him? I should say so! *(Proudly)* He's my son, actually.
Ella	No!
Mary	Yes. Even famous people on local radio have mothers, you know.
Ella	But if you're his mother, why . . .
Mary	Go on?
Ella	Nothing.
Mary	If I'm a local celebrity's mother, why am I gathering my own firewood? Because I choose to. Just because I've got a well known son doesn't mean I want to live in a forty-bedroomed mansion at Wallywood or somewhere and get waited on. Anyway, I meet such nice people this way. So, are you going to the church tonight?
Ella	I'm not sure . . .
Mary	Well, it's up to you. Just don't be put off by what other people say. Now if you'll excuse me, I must get some more firewood before my back *really* plays up.

Ella	Here – have mine. I can get some more.
Mary	Are you sure?
Ella	Yes. Take it. I'm in no hurry to get back, anyway.
Mary	Thank you – you're a very kind girl. God bless you. Goodbye. And don't forget to go to the church.
Ella	Goodbye. And thank *you*.

Exit MARY.

Ella	Now I'm really up against it – but I couldn't just watch her struggle, could I?

ELLA picks up a few sticks from the floor and exits.

SCENE 3

The Kitchen at Bourton Paidfor Hall.

BARON SPENTUP is checking his accounts and going through a huge pile of bills.

Suggested background music: *Nobody knows the trouble I've seen.*

Baron   Really! This is ridiculous! Those daughters of mine will ruin me!

WANT, WANT, WANT
Tune: *Little Brown Jug*

Baron   It's really not much fun at all
being master of Bourton Paidfor Hall.
Just look at all the things I've got,
and am I happy? Not a lot!

*Want, want, want, spend, spend, spend,
this is a most alarming trend;
want, want, want, spend, spend, spend,
drives a poor baron round the bend.*

Because I've got this country seat,
you'll be thinking that I'm on Easy Street,
I seem to be a wealthy bloke,
but am I happy? What a joke!

I give them all they ask me for,
but all they can do is cry for more.
No matter how my wealth increased,
would I be happy? Not the least!

Baron   *(Calls)* Anaesthesia! Anaglypta!

Heavy, running footsteps offstage. ANAESTHESIA and ANAGLYPTA enter, breathlessly.

Anaesthesia   Yes, Father *dearest*?

Anaglypta   Did you call us, *beloved* Papa?

Baron	It's about money.
Anaesthesia	You're going to give us the advance! Father, you're *wonderful*!
Anaglypta	The best papa in all the world!

They embrace him effusively.

Anaesthesia	I've always said we have such a marvellous father.
Anaglypta	No one could ever want a better!
Baron	*(Struggling free of them)* No, I am *not* giving you another advance.
Sisters	What?!
Baron	I want to know about these bills.
Anaesthesia	But Father, they're nothing.
Anaglypta	Just a few little knick-knacks we bought.
Baron	*(Going through the bills one by one)* Just a few knick-knacks! A hundred cans of extra-firm hairspray.
Anaesthesia	It's cheaper in bulk.
Anaglypta	And it lasted us a whole month.
Baron	Two fifty-gallon drums of anti-wrinkle cream.
Anaesthesia and Anaglypta	*(Pointing to each other)* They're hers.
Baron	Four pairs of diamond-encrusted wellington boots?
Anaesthesia	Two pairs each.
Anaglypta	One to wear, and one to wash.
Baron	Five dozen designer ball-gowns?
Anaesthesia	What else d'you wear to a designer ball?
Anaglypta	You don't want us wearing old clothes in public, do you?

Baron	Well, it's got to stop.
Anaesthesia	Father!
Baron	Either that, or you've got to pay your own way.
Anaglypta	Pay our own way?
Anaesthesia	You mean, *work*?
Baron	Unless you can get someone else to pay your bills.
Anaglypta	But no one loves us like you do!
Baron	Why doesn't that surprise me? I'm not arguing about it. It's time you found some other sucker to support you. You'd better hope that this Josh Christian likes your singing and gives you a job – because I'm cancelling all your storecards.
Anaesthesia	I always said Daddy had a mean streak in him. How did we ever come to be cursed with such a father!
Anaglypta	He's the worst papa in all the world!
Baron	Certainly the poorest. *(Calls)* Salome!

Enter SALOME.

Baron	You're to prepare my daughters' makeup, and help them to apply it. They must look radiantly beautiful tonight.
Salome	How long have I got?
Baron	You two, go and do whatever you women do.

Exeunt ANAESTHESIA and ANAGLYPTA.

Baron	And I'd better go and do some crawling to the creditors.

Exit BARON.

Enter ELLA with some firewood.

Salome	You've been ages! Is that all you've got?

Ella	*(Putting sticks into stove)* It'll have to do – you see, I met this poor woman –
Salome	Never mind that, now. Your father's given me the job of doing your sisters' makeup.
Ella	So?
Salome	Well, I don't know how to do it. You'll have to help me.
Ella	I don't know, either.
Salome	It can't be *that* difficult – if only we had someone to practise on.
Ella	So who do you know that would like their faces painted?
Salome	Can't imagine.
Child in Audience	I would!
Ella	Oh no you wouldn't!
Child in audience	Oh yes I would!
Ella	You go and get the makeup: I'll organise some seats. Now who's going to volunteer?

Exit SALOME who comes back with face-painting kit. ELLA sets out some chairs on the stage facing forward.

There will almost certainly be far too many volunteers for two people to handle, so have some help standing by. Even then, there will obviously be a limit, depending on local circumstances, so have a maximum number in mind.

Salome	It's no good. We're going to have to employ some assistants.
Ella	Anybody out there want a job painting faces?

Get the volunteers organised.

Suggested music: *Liberty Bell.*

Paint the children's faces, making comments from time to time, e.g:

> I bet your mum never knew you could look like this! Well, just as long as she doesn't blame me.
>
> I think I'm getting better at this, you know.
>
> Of course, these children are easy. I mean, they're good looking to start with. When it comes to Anaesthesia and Anaglypta . . .
>
> I was enjoying myself until you mentioned them.

Include general banter, based on the actual people involved: interests, personalities, parents' occupations, etc.

Salome	There! That's not bad for a beginner. How're the rest of them?
Ella	This one's OK, I think.
Salome	You are going home by car, aren't you?
Ella	If any of you are walking, just don't come up on anyone suddenly, that's all.

Heavy footsteps offstage.

Salome	They're coming! Off you go, all of you! Hurry!

Children go back to their seats and volunteers help clear the stage, leaving just two chairs facing away from the audience.

Enter ANAESTHESIA and ANAGLYPTA.

Anaesthesia	I hope you're ready, because we mustn't be late at the party.
Salome	We're ready.
Anaglypta	*(Pointing to ELLA)* I'm not having that horrible girl touching me – she's a sinner, she is!
Ella	Why won't someone tell me what I've done?

29

Anaglypta	I don't want to talk about it.
Anaesthesia	We *never* talk about it.
Salome	No, because the answer amounts to the same as you two put together – a big, round, fat, vacant nothing.
	Well, if Ella doesn't help, I'll have to do both of you, and then you'll be late for the party.
Anaglypta	Oh, all right, but stand at arm's length, and don't breathe heavily.

They sit down, with backs to audience.

Anaesthesia	I hope you know what you're doing.
Salome	Oh, yes. I've got a wonderful plan for you. *(Leans behind them and whispers to ELLA who seems delighted at the plan. They make a start. Conversation continues as they work.)*
Anaesthesia	*(Sings to the tune of 'Daisy, Daisy')* Rich and famous, that's what we're going to be.
Salome	I can't make you up if you're doing that.
Anaesthesia	*(Sulkily)* Well, just get on with it, then.
Salome	Perhaps we should do this for them regularly – keep them quiet for five minutes.
Anaglypta	You keep at arm's length, Ella! Remember?
Ella	Now you've made me smudge your makeup!
Anaglypta	Insolent girl!

The session continues until the sisters' faces are painted as clowns.

Possible music: Liberty Bell.

Ella	I think they're about done, now.
Salome	Let's see, twenty minutes on gas mark 7. Yes, I should think so.

Anaesthesia	Cheeky child! Well, don't just stand there. Get me a mirror!
Ella	*(Horrified)* Mirror? You actually want to see what you look like?
Salome	Don't worry. Here are some I prepared earlier.

SALOME produces two 'mirrors' with pictures of extremely beautiful women's faces stuck to them, and shows them to the audience before holding them in front of the sisters.

Anaesthesia	Is that the best you can do?
Anaglypta	Not very impressive, is it?
Anaesthesia	Not my usual standard of exquisiteness, at all.
Anaglypta	Still, we've no time to change it now. It will just have to do.
Salome	Are you going to show the boys and girls what you look like.
Anaesthesia	Oh, I don't think *they* want to see.
Ella	Oh yes they do!
Anaglypta	Oh no they don't!

The Ugly Sisters are eventually persuaded to show their faces to the audience. They are made up as clowns. Then they catch sight of each other.

Sisters *(In unison)*	Ooh! You've made her more beautiful than me.
Ella	No we haven't, honestly.
Salome	No, that's true, neither of you is beauti – any more beautiful than the other.
Ella	Anyway, you've got to go or you'll be late.
Anaesthesia	The horrible one's right. We'll have to go, Anaglypta dear, and just hope it all works. And if we don't end up as singing stars, it'll be worse for both of you.

Salome	I'm not arguing with that.
Anaesthesia	Come on, dear. Let's go and dazzle.

Exeunt ANAGLYPTA and ANAESTHESIA.

ELLA starts to cry.

Salome	Ella! What on earth's the matter.
Ella	Oh, I'm just disappointed. I met this woman in the woods who turned out to be Josh's mother, and she said I ought to go to the church, and he'd be nice to me. That's all I really want, for someone to be nice to me – someone other than you, that is. For a moment I really thought – well, it's too late now.
Salome	Nonsense! Of course you can go.
Ella	But there's no time for me to get ready.
Salome	Don't be silly!

SALOME erects a screen for ELLA to change behind.

Ella	I haven't got a nice dress.
Salome	No, but one of Anaesthesia's should fit if I put some big tucks in it. I'll go and get some for you to choose from. Meanwhile you get out of that old thing. Hurry!

ELLA goes behind the screen, and SALOME exits.

Enter MARY.

Mary	Ella? Are you here? Oh, I do hope I've got the right house.
Ella	I'm behind here.

Enter SALOME carrying a beautiful dress.

Salome	Hello, can I help you?
Mary	I'm Mary – a friend of Ella's. We met in the woods.

Ella	Oh yes, she told me. 'Scuse me a minute while I give Ella this dress.
Mary	*(Peering behind the screen)* Ella, put your usual dress back on and come here.
Ella	But I haven't –
Mary	Don't argue!
Ella	Oh, all right!
Salome	I don't want to be rude, Mary, but –
Mary	I'm sorry to seem interfering but I know Josh well, and believe me *(Pointing to the dress SALOME is carrying) that* is *not* the way to impress him.

ELLA emerges from behind screen.

Ella	What's going on?
Mary	It's very simple, Ella – you're going to the party, and you're going just as you are.

YOU'RE LOVELY AS YOU ARE
Tune: *Down by the riverside*

Mary	You don't need any fancy dress: you're lovely as you are, you're lovely as you are, you're lovely as you are, you've got nobody to impress, God knows that you're a star, you're lovely just as you are. In God's very image, you are made, in you is displayed your Creator's face. So let's see you hold your head up high, look me in the eye, you are a work of grace!

>   Being human is no disgrace,
>   you're lovely as you are,
>   you're lovely as you are,
>   you're lovely as you are,
>   you've got no need to paint your face,
>   and all that la-di-da,
>   you're lovely just as you are.

Mary and Salome *In God's very image, you are made,*
in you is displayed
your Creator's face.
So let's see you hold your head up high,
look me in the eye,
you are a work of grace!

Dialogue:

Ella	You're right! I'm no worse than anyone else at the church. And I'm going to go. As I am!
Mary	Well said! Now get over there and enjoy the evening!
Ella	Just a minute! *(Dashes offstage)*
Mary	*Now* what's she doing?
Salome	You never can tell with Ella.

Enter ELLA carrying a bottle.

Ella	Just a little gift for Josh.
Salome	But that's –
Ella	Yes – the perfume my mother left me.
Salome	Well, Josh is pretty liberated, but . . . perfume!
Ella	It's the only thing of value I've got.
Mary	It's a lovely thought. Josh will appreciate it
Salome	You always swore you'd never use it.
Ella	I think Mum would approve of this. Well, wish me luck.

Mary   (*Hugging her*) All right, but you won't need it.

Salome   (*Hugging her*) Go on!

Exit ELLA.

Salome   I hope we've done the right thing.

Mary   Trust me. Now, while I'm here is there anything I can help with?

Salome   How are you at making beds?

Mary   Try me.

Exeunt.

SCENE 4

The church.

Sign on wall: 'The perfectly Pious Christian Fellowship presents JOSH CHRISTIAN. No Smoking, Sinners or Smelly Feet.' A number of guests are standing around. SIMON is holding court to some admiring cronies.

Background Music: *Waltz from Die Fledermaus.*

Crony 1	*Wonderful* evening, Simon!
Crony 2	Absolutely super!
Simon	Yes, I'm glad you're enjoying it. There's certainly a good turnout.
Crony 1	I expect it's Josh's appearance they've come for.
Crony 2	Absolutely super!
Simon	Well, of course one has to invite people like him – he's very popular – but he's not really the sort of person I should invite normally.
Crony 2	Absolutely, Simon. Um – what sort of person *is* he?
Simon	My dear, the man has no moral standards – no respect for our God-given traditions. Just think of the kinds of friends he chooses and you'll see what I mean. Most of them have – let's say, very colourful pasts. And there's not a single decent philosopher among them.
Crony 1	Not our sort of people at all, then, Simon.
Crony 2	Absolutely. Not at all. Super!
Simon	If I had my way, I should make poverty and ignorance criminal offences.
Crony 1	Yes, Simon.
Crony 2	Absolutely, Simon. Super!

Simon	If people can't be bothered to learn and make some sort of success of their lives, they should be punished.
Crony 1	Yes, Simon.
Crony 2	Absolutely, Simon. S – *(SIMON silences him)*
Simon	And I'd have none of this silly liberal nonsense, either – turning prisons into holiday camps. Stick them in solitary, that's what I say, until they have learnt something and made a success of themselves.
Crony 1	Er – yes, Simon.
Crony 2	Absolutely, Simon.
Simon	Oh, yes indeed, given the opportunity I should rid our society completely of empty-headed, frivolous people.

Enter ANAESTHESIA and ANAGLYPTA

Anaesthesia	Coo-ee! Simon!
Anaglypta	Hello there, darling! What an absolutely fabulous evening!
Simon	But unfortunately, as things are . . . Hello, Anaglypta, Anaesthesia, how very good of you to come.
Anaesthesia	Oh, you know we like to be seen in all the best places.
Anaglypta	*(Aside to audience)* But this'll have to do.

Enter JOSH with PIERS, unnoticed by SIMON who continues conversing in mime with the two sisters and cronies.

Josh	This is the place. That's Simon over there.
Piers	Why are we here, Josh? These aren't our kind of people.
Josh	I go where I'm invited, Piers. There are some people who say I shouldn't associate with you, either.
Piers	*(Angrily)* Who! I'll soon sort them out!

Josh	And that's why. You know, Piers, when I'm trying to encourage people to love each other, you don't always help.
Piers	I'm sorry, but look at Simon now. He invites you here, and then ignores you.
Josh	That's his choice, Piers, but I'm here.
Anaesthesia	Ooh, look, dear – Simon, isn't that Josh?
Simon	Oh, yes, I believe it is. Just like him to sneak in without being properly announced. Now, as I was saying –
Anaglypta	Josh! Just the man to be seen with. *(Calls)* Josh! Coo-ee! Over here!
Piers	Oh, no! Perhaps being ignored isn't so bad after all.
Josh	Don't be unkind, Piers. Let's go and talk to them.

PIERS and JOSH go over to where the sisters and SIMON are standing. They mime conversation.

Enter ELLA who sees the assembled company and falters.

Ella	*(To audience)* Oh, dear! Why did I come here? I'm not good enough to come to this place.
Child in audience	Oh yes you are!
Ella	Oh no I'm not!

(Children respond appropriately: keep this exchange going ad lib).

Ella	Perhaps if I just sneak up and give Josh my present. Dare I do that?

Encouraged by the children, ELLA tentatively approaches JOSH. If the children are responding well, this could be drawn out by several 'false starts' and second thoughts. Eventually, ELLA becomes desperate.

Ella	I shouldn't have come! He's really special and I'm so evil! How could I have been so stupid!

JOSH catches sight of ELLA and goes to speak to her. At the same time, ANAGLYPTA and ANAESTHESIA see her and bear down upon her.

Ella I'm sorry! I'm so sorry! Shouldn't have come – brought you a present – forgive me – silly horrible girl – *(She turns to go, trips and spills the perfume over JOSH.)* I'm sorry! I'm sorry! Forgive me. Ohhhh! *(She rushes out, discarding the empty bottle.)*

Josh Wait! Don't go! *(She goes)* That poor woman!

Simon *(To cronies)* See what I mean? He actually encourages that sort of person, you know.

Anaesthesia I'll kill her!

Josh You know her?

Anaesthesia Who? Me? Never saw her before!

Anaglypta As if we'd know anyone like that! What sort of people do you think we are?

Josh Of course. Silly of me! Fancy thinking *you* would know anyone like that!

Anaglypta *(Aside to ANAESTHESIA)* He likes me.

Anaesthesia Hands off!

Josh I must find her.

Anaglypta Oh, you don't want to know her. Now – where are the auditions?

Anaesthesia She's a terrible, horrible, absolutely disgusting person. Now, about my contract . . .

Josh She isn't disgusting at all.

Anaglypta Oh yes she is.

JOSH encourages the children to join in and the two sisters argue fiercely with them until JOSH intervenes.

Josh So, what has she done, then?

Anaesthesia	I don't want to talk about it.
Anaglypta	We *never* talk about it.
Piers	Give me five minutes, Josh – I'll get it out of them.
Josh	Piers, I'm not the least interested in whatever these two are accusing her of. I just think it's significant that they can't actually tell me what it is. Now, the best thing you can do is help me find her so that I can help her.
Simon	Help her! See what I mean? The man's a namby-pamby liberal. *(To JOSH)* The people you should be helping are the good law-abiding people like us who are intimidated by the likes of her.
Josh	Something tells me you can cope. *(He picks up the discarded bottle and sniffs)* This is a very distinctive perfume she's spilled on me, and I bet her hands will smell of it for a long time. Right! I'm not going to rest, eat or sleep until I've found her. Come on, Piers, let's leave these little people to their little party and go and find someone important – the woman whose perfume matches this one.

Exeunt JOSH and PIERS.

Anaesthesia	Well! You could knock me down with a bulldozer!
Anaglypta	I've come over all peculiar!
Anaesthesia	Ooh, that perfume!
Anaglypta	*(Nudges ANAESTHESIA)* Can you take me home, dear – I've come over all faint.
Anaesthesia	What?
Anaglypta	*(Takes her aside and speaks in a stage whisper)* We've got to get back and get Ella out of the way before Josh comes snooping around.
Anaesthesia	Why?
Anaglypta	Why d'you think!

Anaesthesia	Oh! Right! *(Faints extremely dramatically).*
Anaglypta	*(Staggering as she catches her)* Oh! Oh dear! I say, could any of you kind gentlemen help me?
Simon	*(Pretending not to notice)* Perhaps we should continue on the terrace. Come on, everybody.
Anaglypta	*(In a stage whisper to ANAESTHESIA)* What are you after – an Equity card or something?

Exeunt ANAESTHESIA and ANAGLYPTA to one side, everyone else to the other.

Simon	*(As he leads the guests out)* The terrace is always pleasant at this time of year.

SCENE 5

The kitchen at Bourton Paidfor Hall.

ELLA is being comforted by SALOME.

Ella Oh, Salome, it was awful! As soon as I got there I remembered how horrible I am, and everyone was looking at me, and –

Salome Hey, calm down! Did you give Josh the present?

Ella I panicked, and ended up spilling it all over him. I made a terrible fool of myself.

Salome I'm sure you didn't. Did she, children?

Salome Anyway, what did Josh say?

Ella I didn't give him time. I just ran out. I was feeling so guilty, and so silly, I just wanted to get away from there. Now, Anaesthesia and Anaglypta are *really* going to be horrible to me.

Heavy footsteps off.

Ella Oh no! Here they come, now!

Enter ANAESTHESIA and ANAGLYPTA

Anaesthesia (*To ANAGLYPTA in a stage whisper*) Now don't forget, dear, be nice to the brat.

Anaglypta Ella, *darling*! Whatever's the matter?

Salome Fat lot you care.

Anaesthesia Oh yes we do!

Salome Oh no you don't!

Anaglypta Oh yes we do!

Anaesthesia Such a pity you didn't stay!

Ella	What?
Anaglypta	Still, you didn't lose anything really. Josh isn't your type.
Anaesthesia	Nobody's type, really. I pity anyone who's connected with him.
Anaglypta	You had a narrow escape there.
Ella	But I didn't want anything from him. I just wanted him to like me, that's all.
Anaesthesia	But my dear, you don't need him – *we* like you!
Anaglypta	We *love* you.
Salome	You're after something.
Sisters	Oh no we're not!
Anaglypta	We just want to be nice to our dear little sister who's not happy.
Anaesthesia	Tell you what, dear, why don't you take this *(Gives her some money)* and go and buy yourself something really nice? Take your time.
Anaglypta	Have the day off. *(Gives her some money.)*
Anaesthesia	Aren't you due for a holiday?
Salome	Now I *know* you're up to something.
Anaesthesia	*(Gives SALOME some money)* You go with her, dear.
Anaglypta	Yes, you deserve a day off, too. Have a wonderful time. Well, off you go!
Anaesthesia	Go on. We've got no time to lose.
Anaglypta	She means *you've* got no time to lose.
Salome	There's something I'm missing here.
Ella	I don't care about that – let's strike while the iron's hot!

Exeunt ELLA and SALOME.

Anaesthesia   Right! Come on, dear, we've got to find that perfume.

Anaglypta   But it won't be in the kitchen!

Anaesthesia   Of course it'll be in the kitchen! Since when did Ella use any other part of the house. *Horrible* child! Ugh!

Anaglypta   *(To audience)* Don't you go standing up for her. She's a dreadful, sinful child.

Audience   Oh no she isn't!

Anaglypta   Oh yes she is!

Anaesthesia   We haven't got time for all that – let's get on.

They search around the kitchen, opening bottles and jars and smelling them, rejecting each one as they do so.

Anaglypta   *Now* what?

Anaesthesia   It must be here somewhere.

Anaglypta   Perhaps that was all there was.

Anaesthesia   Oh, no! She wouldn't use the only bottle. What kind of person gives away all they've got? Certainly not horrible children like her.

Anaglypta   Well, we've checked every bottle.

Anaesthesia   Perhaps she mixed some together. Get some bowls and let's get cracking!

ANAGLYPTA goes offstage and comes back with an assortment of bowls. They start mixing the various liquids together, sniffing each one as they do so and scowling in disgust.

Enter BARON SPENTUP.

Baron   What are you two doing back so soon?

Anaesthesia   We just couldn't bear to be away from our darling father.

Anaglypta   Or to leave little Ella doing all the chores.

They return to their work.

Baron   So what are you doing with all this?

Anaglypta   *(Angrily)* We're trying to make perfume, you silly old man.

Anaesthesia   *(Covering up for her)* Ha! ha! Isn't she a wag, Father dear! We're trying to make a special kind of perfume that Josh likes, so that he'll like us.

Baron   Oh, I see. Well, my first wife used to have some really beautiful perfume.

Anaglypta   Where is it?

Anaesthesia   I'll give you anything for it.

Baron   No good asking me. She gave the very last bottle of it to Ella, just before she died, and I never found out where Ella kept it.

Anaglypta   Ella!

Anaesthesia   That horrible child!

Anaglypta   She doesn't deserve nice things . . .

Audience   Oh yes she does!

Anaglypta   Oh no she doesn't!

Anaesthesia   Never mind all that! Tell me, Father dear, was the perfume in a . . . *(Describes bottle)*

Baron   Yes, that's it.

Anaglypta   And you're sure it was the very last bottle.

Baron   Oh, absolutely, but I've no idea where it is now.

Sisters   *(Wail)* We have!

Enter MARY.

Mary	Excuse me . . .
Anaglypta	*(Roughly)* Who are you?
Anaesthesia	*(Roughly)* What d'you want?
Mary	I was looking for Ella.
Anaglypta	You mean *Sinner* Ella
Anaesthesia	Horrible child!
Mary	What's she done?
Anaglypta	I don't want to talk about it.
Anaesthesia	We *never* talk about it.
Baron	Why are you looking for her?
Anaglypta	Don't talk to her, Father.
Anaesthesia	She's obviously a sinner, too.
Mary	Well, it's not so much me as my son who's looking for her.
Anaglypta	Oh, yes . . .
Anaesthesia	Likes girls like her does he, this son of yours?
Mary	But Ella's a lovely girl.
Sisters	Oh no she isn't!
Mary	*(Sadly)* Well, I suppose I'll just have to tell Josh to look elsewhere.
Baron	Did you say Josh?
Anaesthesia	Your son?
Baron	My dear lady, why didn't you say so? Please forgive my daughters their rudeness.

THAT'S THE WRONG WAY TO TALK TO MARY
Tune: *It's a long way to Tipperary*

Baron That's the wrong way to talk to Mary,
it's the wrong way to speak!
That's the wrong way to talk to Mary,
it's a very poor technique!
Don't bite the hand of fortune,
don't forget your place,
that's the wrong, *wrong* way to talk to Mary,
a woman of grace.

He turns sycophantically to MARY.

Baron The mother of Josh is always welcome here. *(To ANAGLYPTA)* Anaglypta, get the lady a chair!

Mary *(Coldy)* No, please don't trouble – I prefer to stand.

Anaesthesia I hope you'll forgive our little misunderstanding.

Anaglypta We love our little joke you know.

Anaesthesia And Ella's got a wonderful sense of humour. We're always pulling her leg.

Audience Oh no you're not!

Anaesthesia and Anaglypta Oh yes we are!

Anaglypta It's so sad that you've missed her.

Anaesthesia She's emigrated, you know.

Baron *(Puzzled)* I didn't know that.

Anaesthesia *(With effusive sympathy)* Poor Father.

Anaglypta We wanted to shield you from it.

Anaesthesia Ungrateful girl – after all you've done for her!

Anaglypta The love we've shown her!

Mary Are you *sure* she's emigrated?

Anaesthesia	Absolutely.
Anaglypta	It's very sad.
Mary	Where to?
Anaesthesia	St Martin's.*
Anaglypta	Now, that's *really* sad.
Mary	Well, wherever she is, Josh is determined to find her. He'll search her out, I've no doubt.
Anaglypta	What? Even there?
Mary	He'll go to every house in every street until he does. Here he comes now. I'll just slip out quietly – I don't want to get in the way.

Exit MARY.

BARON SPENTUP is wiping his eyes.

Anaglypta	What's the matter, now?
Baron	Ella! Gone! My poor little Ella!
Anaesthesia	Fat lot he cares: he just wants his meals cooked.
Anaglypta	We haven't got time for this.
Anaesthesia	Don't worry, Father, she'll be back before you know it.
Baron	How d'you know that?
Anaglypta	Because horrible little sinners like her always turn up, that's why. Now we've got to get on – or get the perfume on, anyway. Father, dearest, would you like to go and grieve somewhere else? Women's stuff, you know.
Baron	Oh – yes – all right, then.

Exit BARON.

Anaglypta	Right. Perfume!

*Use the name of a nearby church or school which in less enlightened days would have been seen as a rival.

Anaesthesia	But which one? What did Ella's perfume smell like?
Anaglypta	Only one thing for it – a little dab of each should do it.

They splash the various concoctions copiously on themselves, putting different perfumes on different hands, behind ears etc.

Suggested music: *Dance of the Hours.*

Anaesthesia	Here they come!

Enter PIERS.

Piers	Right! Now pay attention everybody –
Anaglypta	Oh, get him!
Anaesthesia	Only if I can't get Josh.

Enter JOSH.

Josh	Excuse me, may I come in?
Anaglypta	Ooh, what a gent!
Anaesthesia	Clearly, a man of our station and breeding.
Josh	I do apologise: Piers is a bit impetuous but he doesn't mean to be rude. I don't know whether you've heard, but I'm trying to trace a particular lady.
Anaglypta	*(Nudging ANAESTHESIA and winking)* Oh, well, it can't be you then, can it? You're not in the least particular.
Anaesthesia	Speak for yourself.
Anaglypta	How wonderful to see you. Would you like a drink?
Piers	I'd prefer a fire exit!
Josh	I'll come straight to the point. *(Holding out perfume bottle)* Do you recognise this perfume?
Anaglypta	But of course I do – I wear it all the time.
Anaesthesia	Here, let me. *(Takes bottle and sniffs deeply)* Oh, no you don't – *I* use that.

Anaglypta   Oh no you don't!

Anaesthesia   Oh yes I do!

Josh   Excuse me. May I? *(Takes ANAGLYPTA's hand and bends to sniff the back of it.)*

Anaglypta   Ooh, what a charmer!

Anaglypta   Ooh, what a performance!

Josh   Ooh, what a p – p – particularly unusual fragrance!

Anaglypta   You mean –

Josh   No, not the same at all.

Anaglypta   Oh, but on the other hand – I'm wearing another scent.

Josh   *(Sniffs other hand)* Scent *away* is what that one should be.

Enter SALOME, unnoticed by everyone else. She stops to watch what is going on.

Anaesthesia   Try me, Josh! I smell much nicer than her.

Anaglypta   Yes, to another frog.

Anaesthesia   Coming from a toad like you –

As JOSH, in mime, calms the sisters and begins to smell ANAESTHESIA's hands, SALOME speaks to the children.

Salome   I knew they were up to something, getting us out of the way like that. I'm going to get Ella. You make sure Josh doesn't leave here.

Exit SALOME.

Piers   Come on, Josh! We know it wasn't one of these two, anyway.

Josh   No, but they may still want to –

Anaglypta   Oh, we would, we would!

Anaesthesia	We thought you'd never ask!
Piers	But Josh, they're quite unsuitable. We don't want people like –
Josh	People like what, Piers?
Piers	*(Drawing Josh aside, confidentially)* Look, Josh, we've already got Jud in the group, and he can't be trusted an inch –
Josh	Piers . . .
Piers	Then there's Matt – winner of the Crooked Accountant of the Year award three years in succession. We've got enough oddballs without taking on these two as well.

JOSH and PIERS continue to talk in mime, while the SISTERS take over the main roles.

Anaglypta	Look, dear, I think they like us.
Anaesthesia	I'll just give him a quick flash of my tessitura.
Anaglypta	D'you think you know him well enough?
Anaesthesia	*(Caterwauls horribly)* La, la, la, la, la, la, la, la, la, la . . .
Anaglypta	Hush, dear – they're coming over.
Piers	All right, if you really want to, you can join our group.
Anaesthesia	I knew once you heard my voice . . .
Josh	Voice?
Piers	You mean – you want – *to sing*?
Anaglypta	Of course! What else?
Josh	I'm sorry; we've obviously created a misunderstanding. We meant you could help with our *social* project.
Anaesthesia	What project's that, then?
Piers	You wouldn't like it.

Josh	*(To PIERS)* That's for them to decide, Piers. *(To the sisters)* We work with disadvantaged people, *(The sisters look apprehensive)* helping the poor – *(The sisters wince visibly.)*
Piers	caring for the terminally ill –
Josh	– and we're starting off a new project focusing on mental health.

ANAGLYPTA and ANAESTHESIA start back in horror.

Anaesthesia	Nutters!
Anaglypta	Fruit-cakes!
Sisters	Crazy people with bizarre behaviour!
Anaglypta	I've just remembered an urgent appointment.
Anaesthesia	Gotta go and have my warts waxed.
Anaglypta	Do excuse us. Bye.

They back away, smiling sweetly. JOSH turns to PIERS and starts to mime conversation.

The SISTERS look at one another and freeze in horror as realisation dawns. They gingerly approach JOSH again.

Anaesthesia	Excuse me, just one moment. We were just wondering . . .
Anaglypta	These poor unfortunate people . . .
Anaesthesia	You do take precautions when you're with them?
Josh	Precautions?
Anaglypta	Oh, nothing elaborate – just mask, gloves, sterile gown, that sort of thing.
Josh	Whatever for?
Anaglypta	He doesn't!

Anaesthesia	Do you, er, – that is – you wouldn't would you – I mean –
Piers	Oh, get on with it!
Anaglypta	You don't actually *touch* them?
Josh	Why not?
Anaesthesia	He does!
Anaglypta	And now he's touched *me*!
Anaesthesia	He held my hand!
Anaglypta and Anaesthesia	We're doomed!

ANAGLYPTA and ANAESTHESIA panic and rush off stage.

Josh	That's sad.
Piers	A narrow escape I call it.
Josh	For a minute there, I thought they might join us.
Piers	Exactly.
Josh	You shouldn't be unkind, Piers.

Enter ANAGLYPTA and ANAESTHESIA stealthily, pushing an unwilling BARON SPENTUP in front of them. PIERS and JOSH continue to converse in mime, not noticing them. The SISTERS and the BARON speak in stage whispers.

Baron	He looks all right to me. Are you sure he's a kidnapper?
Anaesthesia	I tell you, he's after Ella.
Anaglypta	And if you don't get rid of him, he'll take her away.
Anaesthesia	And you know what that means, don't you?
Anaglypta	D'you know what a *real* kitchen maid earns, these days?

BARON looks horrified, staggers and has to be supported.

Baron All right, then, but I don't like it.

Exeunt ANAESTHESIA and ANAGLYPTA. BARON goes over to JOSH and PIERS.

Baron Welcome to my humble house.

Piers Humble! We know people who'd be proud to own a corner of it.

Baron Oh, it looks impressive, I know, but with the cost of upkeep, and the trouble getting staff – times are very hard for the rich, these days, you know.

Josh Then, I'm just the person you need. I've got the answer to all your problems.

Baron A donation?

Josh No, an invitation. If this is such a burden, why not sell it? You could give the money to the poor.

Baron Oh, but the market's not very good at present, you know. Not a good time to be selling. Anyway, I'd only have to buy somewhere else to live – and it's not a good time for buying, either.

Josh You can come and live with me.

Baron You got a good place?

Josh Wonderful! Beautiful views, extensive grounds, and no repair bills. And I never have any trouble with the servants, because there aren't any.

Baron No servants?

Josh No servants, no walls, no roof, no mortgage. Mind you, it gets a bit cold sometimes but we usually manage to find a shop doorway if it rains.

Baron You're winding me up.

Josh I never wind people up, Baron.

Piers They work better if you don't.

Baron	Well anyway, it's nice of you to invite me, but I think I'll stay here. We poor landowners have a social responsibility, you know. Now, was there anything else?
Josh	Is there anyone here we haven't met yet?
Baron	I live here alone, with my two lovely daughters. No, there's no one else.
Audience	Oh yes there is!
Baron	Oh no there isn't!
Piers	Come on, Josh, we're wasting our time here.
Baron	Let me push you – I mean show you – out.
Josh	You're quite sure there's no one else?
Baron	No one at all.
Audience	Oh yes there is!
Baron	Oh no there isn't!
Josh	The children over there seem to think otherwise.
Piers	Oh, ignore them Josh. They're just a bunch of silly children.
Audience	Oh no we're not!
Piers	Oh yes you are!
Josh	Well, children, *is* there anyone else here?
Children	Yes
Baron	You're a load of little liars, you are!
Children	Oh no we're not!
Baron	Oh yes you are!
	etc.

Enter ELLA and SALOME.

Salome	I think this is who you're looking for, Josh.

Baron	That's torn it!
Ella	I'm sorry. I didn't really want to trouble you. Salome made me. I'll just go away somewhere.
Josh	What's the matter? Why are you afraid of me?
Ella	Because you're good.
Salome	I keep telling her that's nonsense.
Piers	You watch your tongue.
Salome	I didn't mean –
Josh	*(Kindly)* I know what you meant. *(To ELLA)* Come here. *(She hesitates)* There's really nothing to be afraid of – or ashamed of.

Enter ANAESTHESIA and ANAGLYPTA.

Anaesthesia	Don't you move another step. Oh, thank goodness we're in time!
Anaglypta	You really don't want her, Josh.
Josh	Why?
Anaesthesia	Because she's a little slut, that's why.
Anaglypta	But she's *our* little slut. And we'd hate to see her go.
Josh	I get it. She's your little slut who's nicely under control, waits on you hand and foot and whom you've managed to convince that she's not fit for anything else.
Anaesthesia	As if we'd do a thing like that!
Anaglypta	The very idea!
Baron	*(Weakly)* They don't mean any harm, you know. They're lovely girls, really. You'd like them if you got to know them.
Piers	I think I'd like them better if I knew them less.
Josh	Come here, Ella. Would you hold out your hand?

Anaesthesia	Don't trust him, Ella. I've met his sort before. You don't want to be friends with anyone who'd hold *your* hand!
Anaglypta	Horrible child!
Josh	You keep saying these things, but you won't tell me what she's done.
Anaglypta	I don't want to talk about it.
Anaesthesia	We *never* talk about it.
Baron	We talk about other things, though. We talk about religion a lot.
Josh	That explains a great deal. *(He takes ELLA's hand and sniffs it.)*
Anaglypta	Ooh, I can't bear to look.
Anaesthesia	Tell me when it's over!
Josh	That's it! That's the perfume! So it was *you* who came to the church.
Anaglypta	Without an invitation!
Anaesthesia	In those horrible clothes!
Anaglypta	And without going to confession first!
Both	Oh, the shame!
Josh	Ella, would you like to help with our new project?
Ella	Well, I don't know. I can't leave Salome here alone.
Baron	*(Wounded)* Oh, but you can leave your father, I suppose!
Anaesthesia	After all we've done for you!
Anaglypta	The love we've showered on you!
Anaesthesia	The things we've put up with for you!

Anaglypta	The shame we've endured!
Sisters	And all for love!
Piers	Is the cabaret over, now?
Josh	If Salome wants to come as well, that's no problem. But you ought to know what you're taking on.

THE FOXES HAVE HOLES
Tune: *Loch Lomond.*

Josh	The foxes have holes, and the birds have their nests, but the streets are all we can offer. The stars are our roof, and our carpets are of stone,
Piers	and there's nothing but love in our coffers.
Refrain: **Josh**	*Oh come, walk with me on the journey of faith – bring the doubts and the fears that beset you, and trust in the God in whose image you are made, who will never forsake or forget you.*
	Although it may seem, in the world we all know, that the wealthy have all of the power, yet love is the pow'r, in the kingdom of our God, that will bring hope and justice to flower.
Refrain: **Josh**	
Josh	And yet we must live in the world as it is, by the hope and values of heaven, in joy and in sorrow, in laughter and in pain, and forgiving till sev'nty times seven.

ELLA and SALOME join in the final refrain with JOSH, slightly adapting the words:

> *Yes, We'll walk with you, on the journey of faith, through the doubts and the fears that beset us, and trust in the God in whose image we are made, who will never forsake or forget us.*

Josh (*To BARON and the SISTERS*) Are you sure you won't come, too?

Anaglypta After you've made it sound so wonderfully attractive, what can we possibly say, except . . . (*All three, in chorus*) NOT PERISHING LIKELY!

Piers Phew! That was a close one.

Ella (*Approaching ANAESTHESIA*) So . . . goodbye, then.

BARON, ANAESTHESIA and ANAGLYPTA turn their backs.

Josh Don't worry. You can come back and visit them whenever you like. And if ever you change your mind, I won't stop you coming home.

Ella Goodbye, everybody.

Exeunt, JOSH, PIERS, SALOME and ELLA.

Anaglypta Have they gone?

Anaesthesia Is it safe to turn round?

They turn round.

Baron *Now* what are we going to do?

Anaglypta Do?

Baron Well, we've got to do something.

Anaesthesia I'll think about it after dinner.

Anaglypta Dinner! I hadn't thought of that!

Anaesthesia Who's going to cook our dinner?

Baron Well, you can hardly expect a frail old man like me to do it. Or to gather firewood, or make the beds, or do the washing, or clean the stove, or –

Anaesthesia That's not work for respectable people.

Baron Of course not. That's why we need sinners. Every home should have one.

Anaglypta	*(Rounding on ANAESTHESIA)* This is all your fault.
Anaesthesia	What?
Baron	She's right. It's all your fault.
Anaesthesia	How d'you work that out?
Baron	Never mind that – just get on with it.
Anaglypta	I want the stove gleaming, the table scrubbed, and the dinner served. And after that you can give the bathroom a good clean and muck out the chickens. *(She shudders)* Ooh, you horrible, wicked person.
Anaesthesia	Me? What have I done?
Baron and **Anaglypta**	We don't want to talk about it.

Exeunt BARON and ANAGLYPTA.

Anaesthesia	Just a minute! Josh! Wait for me! *(Rushes off after JOSH.)*

THE GIDDY LIMIT